PANDEMONIUM

BY THE SAME AUTHOR

physical
playtime

PANDEMONIUM

Andrew McMillan

CAPE POETRY

1 3 5 7 9 10 8 6 4 2

Jonathan Cape, an imprint of Vintage, is part of the Penguin Random House group of companies whose addresses can be found at global.penguinrandomhouse.com

Penguin Random House UK

First published by Jonathan Cape in 2021

penguin.co.uk/vintage

The authorized representative in the EEA is Penguin Random House Ireland, Morrison Chambers, 32 Nassau Street, Dublin D02 YH68

A CIP catalogue record for this book is available from the British Library

ISBN 9781787333192

Typeset in 11/13 pt Bembo by Jouve (UK), Milton Keynes

Printed and bound in Great Britain by TJ Books Ltd, Padstow, Cornwall

Penguin Random House is committed to a sustainable future for our business, our readers and our planet. This book is made from Forest Stewardship Council® certified paper.

FSC www.fsc.org MIX Paper from responsible sources FSC® C018179

for Ben   always

they's no peace in houses, they's no rest livin' with folks.
Somethin's always livin' with ye

Eugene O'Neill *Desire under the Elms*

CONTENTS

for how many years
had you carried it
before you felt it

how long had it sat
growing as you grew
built of your own skin

tumour   parasite
and itching   itching
until you looked

who was it showed you?
who gave you the key?
your not-self   sick-self

the long worm body
of your blood wrapped
tight around your brain

and you opened up
found you could not shut
no matter how long

you screamed in your bed
panic loosed   bedlam
pandemonium

SO WILL FALL

whose fault?

Paradise Lost Book 3

passion play

open audition to be held
in the corridor of a one-bedroom flat

let me walk you through it first
start in the living room   a slow deliberate

procession to the bathroom   we need someone
with experience of movement   who understands

how best to capture that writhing
across the tiles to try and get the bleach

we'll need someone to play the bleach
someone light enough to pick up   who won't mind

being thrown around   and we'll need
a drummer for the exact sound of a head

banging against a stud partition wall
we need someone for the clothes piled up

in the corner   to be sat in   whilst weeping
someone for the lock   for the nurse down the line

someone for the door

it begins each time with a quiet withdrawal
from the self   as though the body steps back
from its own skin   folds in on itself
and without its wall of bone behind it
the skin becomes too sensitive to touch

and the brain begins to crease
into smaller and smaller squares   making
itself less visible   the way animals
might when under attack   and the washing
piles up in the basket   and the hair isn't

cleaned for days   and each time it dawns on me
too late   what is about to happen
I say something unconsidered   and you lay down
weeping in the hallway   curled up
by the door   like a draught excluder

routine

it's an unusually busy night
for the ambulances   so I check
that you're still lucid   and then get told
to call a taxi to A&E

which is unusually busy
for a weeknight   at 7pm
and so we wait   for hours   get ushered
into the unusual brightness

of the triage room   and then back out
to wait again   as your body attempts
to come to terms with what's inside of it
and they decide it's best to send you home

but then vomiting begins
and the hospital wards are full
unusually overstretched with bodies
of the dying and the not-today-dying

so you are taken to a room
where an old man is crying out in his sleep
and a curtain is drawn between you
I sleep on the tiled floor like a dog

by your bed   at 5am an orderly
comes to take you to a ward   and though
it isn't yet visiting hours
unusually   they allow me to stay

for a while   a text comes through from home
that in the night our new niece arrived
into the world   so much life arriving
every day   too bright   too bright   I let you sleep

for the second night I have left you
sleeping in the hospital   hooked

up to the drip that will dissolve
the small white momentary lapses

that look to overwhelm your body
I stop the taxi early   needing

the walk into the nighttime's squall
the skyscraper   singing its one long metal note

back into the weather   we're told
it's something in the way it's built

a fault of architecture   the natural enters
leaves screaming

my sister says

we tell the children that the mind
is a glass of water   always almost full to the lip
any extra overwhelms it

there is a bucket under the bathroom light
to catch the dripping rain   trouble
seeps through your skin   nightly   the glass filling

until it topples and we try to gather
up the spreading water in our hands

how long we couldn't bring ourselves to say the word

__________ attempt (as in attempt on someone's life)

__________ attempt (as in something you might get
better at as though something
to strive for)

failed __________ attempt (unsuccessful unable letdown)

shiva

for a week after the hospital
the mirrors in our one-bed flat
are covered with spare towels   old jumpers

if I coax you out to walk the park
it is with a woolly hat pulled down
and scarf tied up above your nose

I suppose if you don't look at yourself
you won't see your own inability
to not be here anymore   back home

I think of prayer   each night sitting   wondering
if god sees himself more in the faces
of the wanting-to-be-dead   what is it

that people see in him?   a son   without
dignity   who steps outside of himself
sees the chaos of the world   and shoulders all of it

sometimes   out dancing in a club   you'll start crying
say this place is new   you don't recognise it
and you're not safe here   it's as though you've swum back

to the surface of your body and found yourself scared
of the many-headed animal of the drunken crowd
its growl of bass   its sweat of alcohol and piss

Sexton says *suicides have a special language*
they only ever ask *what tools?*   daily you go looking
for the instruments of your undoing

eyeing up the trees which could take your weight
looking up the effects of drinking weedkiller
and the music keeps getting louder

even with your hands like headphones on your ears
your face   pounding the pillow   the duvet
with one long flourish of the arm   pulled over you

circumstance

when the newsreader looks square at the camera
and says *the death is not being treated as suspicious*
I know what that means when I read that the police
are not looking for anyone else in connection
I am certain that there's only one conclusion
no one for the detective to question
no one for a pithy quote to camera
just this body they will treat as both the witness and the crime
its paling face its hand that found a moment
of serenity in the blade or the rope
or the conductivity of water

some heard it that night as a boom
and then an aftershock of screaming

some heard it as the lightest thud
a toy falling from a high shelf

some heard it only afterwards
in sirens and gossip on TV

some hardly heard anything   a soft pop
like heads being pulled from flowers

you heard when I had to wake you
and tell you and hold you and lie

to you   that I could keep you safe

pill-box

before   I'd only ever seen them at my grandparents'
each day piled high with coloured tablets the size
of my little finger   each morning's handful
a way of distracting the body from its decline
so when your mind wouldn't settle   and you couldn't
remember   we got one too   a little plastic calendar
in the kitchen   at first you hated it
felt it drew too much attention to itself
like an errant child   but eventually
it left the cupboard for the corner of the worktop
where each night it would sit ready   like a packed lunch
and it felt like recovery   a series
of small windows to be opened   to scoop out
brief comfort   until one day you thought it too big
too obvious   and we dug out my grandad's from the deep
of some forgotten box   small   flesh-pink
each day like opening a knuckle on a fist
and inside the white static of all the powdered years
his blood pressure   his heart   and I think we mistook it for love
this closed hand of a pill-box   skinny as a child's wrist
that things are easier to live with if you think
they're smaller   just one mouthful   open wide

one thing the pills mean is that you rarely cum
your body pushes you to the edge
but has learnt to step back   rather than jump

over

that weekend it all fell apart   we fucked
like fresh love   tore into each other
like presents   opened each other up
and what was this anger we'd been given
where did it come from   this rage   this point
where other men might fight   might drive their knuckles
into someone's face again and again
as though trying to reach the other side
we too were led by our blood
needing to see it   bring it back to the surface
like some memory of love

ill again   wanking at ten past three
in the morning   sitting on the closed
lid of the toilet seat   watching something
on my phone   pretending to believe
the emotions of the men on the screen
to force myself to heat   to bring myself
to empty in my hand   or in the bowl
the sweet phlegm of my own longing

so groping back down the landing
as though after a piss   I can lay down
this dumb body   all its lust poured out
tamed of its natural reflex
to grow hard when close to you
I know to help   I must uncouple
from any urge   to sleep   to eat   to love
have only patience   waiting for your mind to rise

what happened

you burst blister after blister
on the foil page of tablets
washed each one down with the champagne
dusty on the shelf since graduation

and ever since   I've been trying
to walk you back to yourself   not knowing
he was dead   I should have let you manumit
from your own mind   should have stood aside   let you go

each year I'm tricked by early spring
the eye of winter   when the grey slips off
and the sun comes through

I rip the tarpaulin back
from the outside chairs   wash off the sludge
and the rotting things that sheltered underneath

the furniture sits naked on the balcony
when the cold front comes back
to punish it

there are days   odd days   when I look at you
and see the man I met when we were young
and you were well   those days   I throw the covers off

leap out of bed

TRAINING

hooking the thumbs through the piece of fabric
like the eye of a needle   I let him
wrap my hands   so tenderly
as though dressing a wound   he tells me
of his injury   how the deeper he squats
his back winks out at the base   how at the start
he couldn't even put his underwear on
or pull up his socks   and when my hands are bound tight
in the cotton and the gloves put on   there is the footwork
come up on that heel   bend that knee   as though
he is teaching me to walk   his own hands
are in pads   held up like paws by his face
in permanent surrender
he counts me in   shouts *left* and *right*
my coordination stumbles   and he smiles
kindly   reminds me always to keep the gloves
at my chin   even though no punch is coming
back at me   and later in the changing-room
as the men play that buzzwire game from childhood
weaving their bodies around each other
to avoid the electric pulse of touch
I watch someone on the machine that gives
an electronic printout of the makeup
of the body   like a till receipt
and I'm sixteen again   back with mum
as she takes me to Boots to weigh me
weekly through my self-imposed starvation
and collects the little rolls of paper
for her purse   like a child catching tokens
from an arcade game   and the thunder rumble
of dropped dumbbells brings me back
to this advent calendar of locker doors

a voice outside that shouts *remember*
the legs before the back before the arms
push up from the ground   thrust   lock it out
because most of this is training
in not letting things come in   *push the knees out*
as you squat   bar borne like a cross along the back
or the warm-up   where a black resistance band
holds tight across the thighs   so your legs
cannot bring themselves together as they want to
and as you try to shake it off   like boxer shorts
in that urgency of sudden lust   you lay on your back
scramble the feet   unhook it from the ankle
and times like that   flat out and sprawling
I know that this could be perhaps my greatest
folly   to think if I made myself stronger
I could save anybody   the way
as I falter on a pull-up   he puts his hands
to my glutes and pushes me   how could I
not have known this touch   that doesn't waver
when it's needed but holds the body tight
keeps it steady   stops anything from falling

SWAN

i

the lake is calm tonight
the moon has dropped white feathers on the water

tonight the lake is calm
the wavelets lap like rustling wings

the lake tonight is calm
but look who is coming in to land

to tear the peace asunder

ii

my first time in water
I was unnaturally good   heavier somehow
so much power inside me
arms forcing the water away
like prising someone's mouth apart
to take out what's inside

only ever more water that comes through

iii

then the year everything was swan

feathers on my pillow   on the floor
wet prints in the hallway where I'd walked
men in white coats   little pellets in their hands
the shadow of my back   curved against the wall

iv

the black swan of debt
the black swan of my own body   of my mum
the black swan of sex
the black swan of the house   of the wall   the loft   the damp
the black swan of rain
the black swan of the dog
the black swan of weddings
the black swan of the neighbours   of him

each one fury-footed in my stomach

v

then the year everything was darkness
                    the red beak of my longing

the wedge of men in flight from club to club
banked in at every bar
loneliness   as though I'm dying of thirst
I think the men must be where water is
I always go face-first to drink

vi

sing a swan of sixpence
a broken-hearted guy
four and twenty whoopers
kept locked up inside
when the door was opened
the swans began to hiss
what is the solution
for such a man as this?
they see you in the living room
saying things are wrong
they see you napping fitfully
when all your strength is gone
your mind is in the puddle now
soaking up the rain
they're coming now to peck at it
your damp and ruined brain

vii   queen

mother   don't eat me
mother   I'm trying so hard to get better
I'm sorry I'm a queer

remember how small I was   mother
newly-hatched cygnet   like a cloud fallen down on the water
now it's only rain mother   so much of it

hitting the lake   bringing it to the boil

viii

I plucked each feather from myself
slight resistance and then a rising-out
like pulling up a weed   when I was bald
I beheld myself in the mirror of the water's edge
my neck looked ridiculous
my eyes the only part of me that still had life
I raised each failed wing   just flesh now
nothing for the wind to get up under
the mirror cracked with the tides
I reared up   I jumped   I watched myself
broken   fall towards myself

UNCIVIL

Newton Heath 2016–20

You think these people do not matter. Then they do.

Sean O'Brien

i

stepping out   brief bloodline
of a comet heading home
unseasonal daffodils
curling up   tricked

by the few good days we've had
and still   this sludge of sodden leaves
ankle-deep down every lane
the knitted pelts of cardigans
strung up to the railings
at the side of the chip shop
the market trader   even though
the market is a carpark now

marking out his territory
with bargain proclamations
we thought we knew dishonesty
but then this decade   burning
itself down to the wick

the wind   turning branch against branch
forcing open the mouths of the bins

ii

I've seen one man dig into his groin
at the metrolink stop   stay standing
as he finds the vein   steps off into himself
I've seen couples pass the spice between them

the dry and heavy smell of it
the way the body slumps but hardens
so they become crumbled statues of themselves
huddled down side streets   and daily now
I see their tents   pitched on scrubland
by the road   or on grass verges
of the lock gates   or hidden between trees
so that when the tram's in motion

it's as though I see them behind bars
I have seen them spread like blood
around a body   from the station
to the central square   to these outskirts
I have never known a sky like this

not scabbed with cloud but   nightly   clear
as though the roof of the world were ripped clean off

iii

I remember seeing the schoolgirls pelted
with petrol bombs as they walked to class
my neighbour telling me   the woman in the house
over the road stabbed her boyfriend in the face

each night their voices bleed out through the bricks
into the street   we sit pretending we are elsewhere
as you tell me of the car that followed your mother home
parked up   and then exploded minutes later
of your old class teacher who shakes and shakes
it's easy to forget that violence
is mostly kept inside   and look   now
the girls are trying to walk to school again

each side of the road   flanked   like a muscular hedge
with men   their voices and their broken glass
and the police   their riot shields and batons
the girls are screaming   the girls are running
the way you usually see people run

from a burning building   not *suffer the little children*
just *really make them suffer*

iv

each morning the walk beyond the workmen
as they line up to change   crouch down as though
they are swimmers and the kerb is the edge
of the ocean   slipping off pumps   lacing up boots

sometimes it's jogging bottoms   shimmied down
replaced by practical canvas things   not clothing
but protection   and always   already
the high-vis   illuminated by their own headlights
and beyond them   and beyond the train depot
they service every day   where single carriages
lay like dormant cattle behind fences
the stucco of the terraces is cracked

so the sides of the houses have branches
and the *Railway Hotel* is no longer
near a railway   and has no beds to speak of
though through the empty ringpull of net-curtain
there is a tinfoil glint of Christmas

and as the day breaks itself apart   on the floor
the hatched egg of an upturned hardhat

v

the new flats which will sit on the corner
of the crossroads have been delayed   the scaffolding
loosens its grip each day   sways like a newborn foal
in the wind   gets clambered by children who use it

to launch the building's own bricks at the road
the half pulled-down half rebuilt body vomiting
itself onto the cars   this is regeneration
the old redressed   made shiny   heightened
except this one stalled for lack of money
the roof too old to fix   the front gone slack
the ground unstable   slipped like a disc
from the spinal column   they'd all already sold

and now the buyers own a square of empty space
the way a creature does when it stakes a claim
on where to sleep   the weather keeps on driving through
the gap-toothed walls   doors that open onto nothing
when they say *delayed* they really mean *held back*

like a man   staggering to his feet
to hurl himself back into the fight

GARDEN

the fields heal everyone

Alexander Lukashenko   March 2020

in the beginning
the dead   like the first flowers
for Adam   were few

enough to name them
but soon   they grew too many
the vast fields of them

GEORGE

1.8.19–1.8.19

i

a pigeon has mistaken our window
for horizon   as we head out
to work we find it   stretched out
as though for flight   asleep
in the garden of its own spilt feathers

still warm   dawn air fresh on its back
as we bag it and bin it   all day
the news is of a mother   shot
in the head as she lay over
the body of her toddler

another mother is to be charged
with manslaughter   because she was shot
in the stomach and her foetus died
come the evening   the yard is still downy
with the soft shrapnel of the bird

ii

no one is sure how we should look after
this sadness   uninvited   unwelcome
for twenty minutes yesterday
my parents sat and watched a hawk
keep lookout from the birdbath

I know it happens   but not to –
my other sister sends me photographs
tiny lashes resting on your eyes
as though they've been stitched shut
it's days before my parents sleep again

their daughter gone to grief
their other daughter stoic
as she collects me in the car
how is everything she'd asked   *not good –*
the car swings like a gate into the driveway

iii

sometimes the world untucks itself   goes feral
gives us rain   a month's worth in a single hour
stress fracture   the dwellings built beneath the dam
must be evacuated   the structure must be
emptied to a stable level   people work all night

with pumps and ropes   with the precision
of surgeons   all night the rain hacks down
in short bursts   like an incessant cough   the dam
buckles   permanently on the edge of failure
some people still refuse removal   hold tight

inside their muggy living rooms   *here's the thing*
mister presenter-of-the-local-news
here's the thing   I'm staying put   I'm waiting
for the clouds   or else that dam   or else myself
to break

iv

a coffin the size of a pillow
your body laid down soft inside
it's early   before the day's procession
of adult cremations   we have this hour
to say goodbye to you   three pews

of your would-have-been family   no speeches
nothing to read from the short blank page
of your life   no anecdotes for comfort
just this ceremony   un-birth   slipping back
behind the heavy folds of curtains

and later   at the wake   the other children
play themselves into exhaustion
pre-verbal   theirs is a language entirely
of gesture   willing us to smile at them
help them when they bump themselves   teach them
how to hold their hands over the place that hurts

v

how should we think of you   dear nephew
except in your entirety
you were not the small hook of a life
which didn't latch   nor the spark from a flint
which didn't ignite   nor the unwanted creature

smoked out of its burrow
you were complete and ready
arriving into the room
an already past-tense thing   lost before
you found your way into the ward

George   I'll tell you
what you'll never get to know
we think we're safe   we think ourselves secure
but life sometimes short-circuits   nature
comes knocking at the door

KNOTWEED

when weeds eat the playhouse, what does that say about the family

Naomi Shihab Nye

how many evenings have I thought the garden done
walked out and seen fresh clumps of weed mithering
the dirt   some people cannot tell the difference
between what should be there and not   I'm one of them
ignorant   till one thing overgrows another
or gets choked   there is always something needing
to be tended   a small salvage down in the muck
I've grown to think if I go out at night
I might catch them at it   but the soil lays still
beneath a harvest moon that is the size
of your sadness   and growing   waxing   until
its whole face peers over at our house   pockmarked skin
like a ploughed field picked clean of all its crops
still   you will not come outside

it's hard at first to comprehend the sleeping man
so horizontal   all through the day   so sleepy
despite the hours spent seemingly at rest
but like a meadow glimpsed from a speeding train   of course
there are permanent convulsions
beneath the topsoil of your matted hair   love   what horses
are at work on you   saddled with the twin desires
to get better and be dead   how loud they are
how heavy   how patient as they sit at either end
of your repose   body stretching to its limits
and your head   and feet   tied up to them
as they toss their fly-scabbed manes towards the ceiling
that whinnying that always sounds like laughter
as you put your hands to your ears   someone shouts out
pull

the neighbour thinks someone is stealing
his chickens   that one has been left high
on a branch in warning   the neighbour
thinks a dog is after his chickens
or someone has trained a dog to steal
and a man is standing in the brook
with a sack   I sigh   say *rumour spreads*
too quickly through this street   another
neighbour asks if we've been growing weed
or if the other neighbours have
where is that smell coming from? they shout
pulling up the floorboards one by one
weeks later   chicken heads like loose golf balls
in the woods   dog tracks in the early snow

sometimes my curiosity is a child
that wants to hunt things   like now   as I lever up
a square of the flagstone path   and find panic
a colony of ants   iron filings scattered
as they grab their young   small white eggs and pupae
and run for cover underground   and in the midst
of all their fizz and tumble   a family
of translucent slugs   slowly rousing themselves
having been curled in on one another   hiding
from the world   as though weary of their energetic
neighbours   and who can blame them
and here I am   picking off their roof and looking
as an ant carries the ghost of its future self
and I close the lid of the path back down onto them

the neighbour says the old man has been dead
so long he's decomposed   no one can tell
what did for him in the end   the kid
over the road says he was murdered
hence the police car   parked as though guarding
someone of importance   a fortnight on
all the windows are open   the tongue
of the garage door rolled back   open mouth
full of boxes   the neighbour comes to say
he has two options for the cockerels
a blacked-out box so they never know dawn
and won't wake up   or else a collar
wrapped around their throat to stop their crowing
to break their necks if they try and scream

working the sockets and the knotted joints
of shrub roots   up and out of the soil
digging through the jumble-sale of glass
and bits of rock that seem to grow beneath
the surface   a worm searching for its severed end
flatlines   then restarts itself   nothing
unexpected as I plant the tree
my parents brought for us   but then my spade
strikes something heavier   folded in the creases
of the earth   nuggets of coal   I ease them out
pitch-black   but still able to reflect
the sunken light   and at once I'm burrowing back
to the fireside of my childhood   how patient
some things must learn to be   before they're useful

it's Pride weekend and once again the city streets
only speak the language of the body
I'd be there   any other year   but death
has emptied me   in a way only the garden
can replenish   so I take my knees to soil
let my hands feel out the fine hairs of roots
you hover   bring me tea   I show you the one
tomato that has tried to weather this changeful month
small green button in its yellow leaves
you give more praise than it deserves   as the robin
sparks its embered chest from branch to branch
I guess a nest but don't see one   where young
and hungry mouths are waiting   for a scrap
of anything to ripen on their tongue

the year of no touch   the garden shaggy
and unkempt   autumn storms having turned leaves
to string   and that night you kissed me
uncertain as drizzle   lips dewed and hungry
and each time I think we've reached the edge of us
together – like that time in the middle
of the Hope Valley   when I made up my mind
to leave you   when the lit windows of each house
the train passed broke my heart
it was lambing season   late but barely dark
innocent marionettes in womb blood
coming out into the night – each time like that
we feel our way back   and coming home late
you greet me as though newly arrived

each evening I go out through the parched grass
to the raspberries and blackberries
reach through the netting to handle each one
in their swelling   ripe as the noses of drunks
I take them between my fingers
twist and pull   carry them back to the house
the neighbour spots me   he has a new trophy
a live-in lad to share the house with his mother
the neighbour walks him   topless and smiling   along
the path at the top of the gardens
he plays with the dog   he doesn't talk much
and I'm thinking of Pozzo   pulling
Lucky behind him   one moment dancing
the next moment still   *it's like he's entangled*

sometimes I go out with an urge to hurt it
put my boot to the soft belly
of rotted stump   and the fungi   unkempt
sprung up from the mossy ground and flung
like scabs across the lawn   sometimes I need
the sound of something pulled up from the roots
and tossed aside   most days I'm out with loppers
to cut down the ambitions of the shrubs   when I
was in school there was a game   to throw
a punch as fast as you could and stop
an inch from someone's face   I tried it
once   with mum   tonight   in the dusk light
a final effort of the muscles   the snapping
crunching sound of something breaking

our dog stretches   crawls slow towards me
like a soldier who's had both his legs blown off
I throw a stuffed rabbit   she fetches   shaking it
as though to put out flames   a hundred years of forced-bred
cuteness cannot dull the instinct   still knowing to go
straight for the throat   she wasn't my idea   you said
you wanted her   I said wait for that wall to come down
the survey said it had bowed the floor   you said it was
the way the house had settled   as though on its knees
but the floorboards   rotten   the garden   needing a gate
the garden slipping from the house into the brook
needed sorting before even thinking of letting life
out there   you woke each night convinced the rooms had shifted
the trees moved closer   you said you could hear the sound of barking

it's summer and the moors are burning   the neighbour
from the other side of the tumbledown fence   says
there are no bones in the soil of the north
the streets are foggy all day with the smoke
all you get is dust   a kind of dark sand
the flames are cantering through the peat bogs
you shout to tell me to shut all the windows   as ash falls
you could trowel through someone's grave and never know
the flames are galloping towards the town
slipping their reins   and then the rain
comes suddenly   and with it the plums from the trees
each one gone to ground   to mulch   stripped bald by vermin
sticky with juice of their own rotting   gone to seed
so come spring   new saplings lick up from the dirt

love   forgive me   most of the time   I can't see
the borders of the garden for the trees
can't tell plant from weed   I didn't know how best
to save you from yourself   how to lead your mind back
up the path to the house of itself   I was gone
too much   and didn't know whether it was best
to let you sleep or take you for a walk   or let
you sit in silence   or encourage you to talk
those years   love   were like trying to sift armfuls of soil
for the tiniest of seeds   and yes   sometimes
I wanted to split and scatter   sometimes
I couldn't stand the screaming anymore   more things
survive in the garden now   the more weeds come down
the more the roses open up their clenched faces

descending into the honeycomb cities
I am returning to ground   already
wetted by the transient rains   all the windows
of our house are wide open   climbing the stairs
is like reaching my face into the fridge
the bedroom is alive with your breathing
the clattering teeth of the blinds   outside
the night is perfectly tuned   slow forcing
of the plum trees and their fruit   buzz of motorbikes
on the road   undressing to land beside you
all night the winds come over us
like intermittent water   Ben   I am not
sure what I mean by this but I'll spend my lifetime
coming home to you

NOTES & ACKNOWLEDGEMENTS

thanks to the following publications where earlier versions of parts of this book first appeared:

Eighty Four Anthology   *Freeman's*   *Granta*   *The New Statesman*   *Wild Court*

'swan' is based on   and written after seeing   Matthew Bourne's reimagining of *Swan Lake*

'garden' was commissioned for the Write Where We Are Now Project by Manchester Metropolitan University

poems on page 13 & 55 have phrases from Anne Sexton either directly quoted or hovering just behind

thanks to Robin   as ever   for his passion and belief

Ben   these poems' first reader   and their most important